This journal belongs to

_____

DAILY
GUIDEPOSTS
JOURNAL

A Year of Reflection

Guideposts
New York, New York

Daily Guideposts Journal

ISBN-10: 0-8249-4873-4
ISBN-13: 978-0-8249-4873-3

Published by Guideposts
16 East 34th Street
New York, New York 10016
www.guideposts.org

Distributed by Ideals Publications, a Guideposts company
2630 Elm Hill Pike, Suite 100
Nashville, Tennessee 37214

Guideposts, Daily Guideposts and *Ideals* are registered trademarks of Guideposts.

Acknowledgments

Every attempt has been made to credit the sources of copyrighted material used in this book. If any such acknowledgment has been inadvertently omitted or miscredited, receipt of such information would be appreciated.

All Scripture quotations, unless otherwise noted, are taken from *The King James Version of the Bible*.

Scripture quotations marked (MSG) are taken from *The Message*. Copyright © 1993, 1994, 1995, 1996, 2000, 2001, 2002 by Eugene H. Peterson.

Scripture quotations marked (NAS) are taken from the *New American Standard Bible*, copyright © 1960, 1962, 1963, 1968, 1971, 1972, 1973, 1975, 1977, 1995 by the Lockman Foundation. Used by permission.

Scripture quotations marked (NIV) are taken from *The Holy Bible, New International Version*. Copyright © 1973, 1978, 1984 International Bible Society. Used by permission of Zondervan Bible Publishers.

Scripture quotations marked (NKJV) are taken from *The Holy Bible, New King James Version*. Copyright © 1997, 1990, 1985, 1983 by Thomas Nelson, Inc.

Scripture quotations marked (NLT) are taken from the *Holy Bible*, New Living Translation. Copyright © 1996. Used by permission of Tyndale House Publishers, Inc., Wheaton, Illinois 60189. All rights reserved.

Scripture quotations marked (NRSV) are taken from the *New Revised Standard Version Bible*. Copyright © 1989 by the Division of Christian Education of the National Council of the Churches of Christ in the U.S.A. Used by permission. All rights reserved.

Scripture quotations marked (RSV) are taken from the *Revised Standard Version of the Bible*. Copyright © 1946, 1952, 1971 by Division of Christian Education of the National Council of Churches of Christ in the U.S.A. Used by permission.

Scripture quotations marked (TLB) are taken from *The Living Bible*. Copyright © 1971 by Tyndale House Publishers, Wheaton, Illinois 60187. All rights reserved.

Cover and interior design by Gretchen Schuler-Dandridge
Cover photo by Istock
Typeset by Aptara

Printed and bound in the United States of America
10 9 8 7 6 5 4 3 2 1

A Daily Guideposts Journal Welcome!

A sweet scene unfolded in the pizzeria where I was having a quick dinner before attending church. It was a spring day in New York City, sunny but chilly; a robust man in his forties, dressed in a polo shirt and plaid shorts, came in with his six-year-old in school clothes, her long blonde hair in a ponytail. Soon she was chatting up a storm in the booth next to me. They ate—two big slices for him, two child-size slices for her—and talked.

"We're on a date," the girl said proudly.

Her dad took a second to answer. "Yeah, I guess so. We're on a date."

"We've never been on a date before. This is the first time."

"Yes," he said. "What would you like to talk about?"

"Well," she paused thoughtfully, "what did you do today at work?"

"I didn't go to work. I met some friends and we went to a baseball game. Our team lost."

"Oh," she said, "I'll bet they'll do better next time."

"Yeah, I'm sure they will. And what did you do today at school?"

And so it went. Father and daughter were taking the time to really be together, sharing and listening, being present, getting to know each other better.

As they left, I heard him say, "So, did you like our date?"

"Yeah! Let's do it more and more!"

Their exchange made me smile. *Why, that's how it is with our Creator,* I thought. *God wants to hear from us. He wants to spend time with us, know how our day went, what we're thinking, what's on our mind. He wants to get to know us and wants us to know Him better too.*

One way to develop and strengthen that bond with God is to spend time together—like that father and daughter—in prayer, in Bible study, in quiet time or in writing in a journal. Yes, journal writing is like having a date with the most important Person in your life . . . God.

Every good gift and every perfect gift is from above, and cometh down from the Father of lights, with whom is no variableness, neither shadow of turning.

—JAMES 1:17

A journal can hold many things: the events of your day; your concerns; your prayers; your list of things to be thankful for; your praises of God; your musings about people you love, strangers you meet, surprises in your day, a beautiful moment in nature, antics from your favorite animal, an illuminating Scripture, an inspiring quote. Maybe you'll start with "Dear God, I've got to talk to somebody" or "Here I am, Lord." In whatever way you choose to begin, your journal can record your sadness or gladness, a disappointment or pleasure, a failure or a success, good times and tough times. It might be a long season of illness and recovery or a broken relationship or lost employment. But with faith as your polestar, your words can be building blocks to rejuvenation and renewal, helping sweep you upward to the next summit of adventure.

You may write a few lines or pages upon pages, or maybe just a single word: *love, scared, trust.* Maybe when words don't come or the pen won't move, there will be a splattering of color: crayons drawing a sun, tree or flower, or an abstract painting of red, yellow and blue splashes, or a collage of paper cutouts glued to the page. Maybe it will be a poem that unfolds from a feeling, or some notes to music your heart hears, or a dream that is a doorway to a new understanding of yourself. Each mark, whether words or image, song or story, is a prayer—an offering, a gift, a stepping-stone toward wholeness, healing or rebirth. Maybe it will appear as a stream of joy and laughter bursting forth as surprise, revealing newfound boldness and bubbling confidence.

Whatever goes into your journal and however you choose to express it, it's yours. Everything you write in your journal helps you to grow deeper in your walk with God, to become more of who you were created to be: a precious child made in God's image; someone God created with love and said, "It is good."

Our Journal Format

Scattered throughout these pages are seventeen devotionals about journals and journal writing taken from *Daily Guideposts* authors over the years. You'll see examples of ways to use your journal and how journaling can bring you closer to yourself, to others and to God. Penney Schwab, a journaler for thirty years, learned to stop grumbling and be more thankful. Elizabeth Sherrill learns from her journal to worry less and to practice thinking only about "this day." Marilyn Morgan King retreats to a cabin with a fireplace to pray and write words of gratitude to God. And *Daily Guideposts* reader Sharon Howard finds old copies of the devotional book in which her grandmother had written about her blessings during a difficult period.

In addition, all the journal pages begin with an uplifting Scripture and end with a personal prayer from a *Daily Guideposts* writer, which expresses a spiritual affirmation of praise, hope, thanks, love, joy, faith and more. Each one will help you keep your thoughts open to the will and guidance of God, and feel His compassion and His protection over your life. Here you'll meet friends such as Marion Bond West, mother and son Pam and Brock Kidd, married couple Julia and Andrew Attaway, Dolphus Weary, Scott Walker, Carol Kuykendall, and more.

How to Begin

- *Set aside a certain time each day.* Is the morning, before you get ready for work or the family awakens, a good time? Is there a free moment or break in your day that's better? Is just before bedtime best, when the house is quiet and so are you?
- *Where is your prayer closet?* Find a calm and quiet place where you can be free from distractions. Many times we read that Jesus went away to pray—in the wilderness, on a mountain, at a lake, on a boat. He knew the importance of a certain place and a time apart. So will you.
- *Date your page.* This is a record of your life-moments and all its seasons—the smooth, the winding, the low, the heights, the bumps and starts along the road.

The timeline will always reveal God "who directs our path" and "never leaves us comfortless."

- *Start writing.* A word, a thought, a sentence and more will tumble forth. What is in your heart? Maybe it's nice; maybe not. Say it anyway. Tell your story. Don't judge, don't censure, trust yourself to God's ever-present, compassionate care. And close with "Thy will be done." It leaves every outcome in the hands of God for whom nothing is impossible.
- *Listen.* Take time to pause and listen to God bringing you an answer, an idea or guidance. "Be still, and know that I am God" (Psalm 46:10).
- *Put away your journal in a private place.* Protect your journal writing by keeping it safe. You may wish to share it with another person, if you choose. It's up to you.
- *Read your journal from time to time:* weekly, monthly, several times a year or on special occasions like birthdays or New Year's. Mark your answered prayers; you'll be amazed. Rejoice in how much you've grown, how much you've overcome. And most of all, see the good gifts of God all around you.

Godspeed!

—TERRI CASTILLO

Daily Guideposts Journal Editor

But true praise is a worthy sacrifice; this really honors me. . . .
—PSALM 50:23 (TLB)

The personal journal I've kept for nearly thirty years began as a challenge. I'd been grumbling about my circumstances, so a friend suggested I write down one thing, every single day, for which I was truly thankful. Even though the first entries were simple, it sometimes took me quite awhile to write, "Thanks, God, for a good night's sleep" or "I praise You for keeping us safe during the hail storm." Later, I began to praise God for answered prayer: "Thank You for Patrick's finding just the right job . . . for guiding the doctor's hand during my neighbor's eye surgery . . . for giving me the right words for today's speech." Gradually the journal became a record of my walk with God. Looking back, I clearly saw His guiding hand, His presence and His leading in every circumstance, whether joyful or difficult.

I was browsing through last summer's entries when the one for August 4 leaped off the page: "Thank You for the rain, but it wasn't as much as we needed." Whoa! That wasn't a prayer, it was a complaint! I read on and discovered a disturbing number of complaint-prayers. When I replaced my car after 197,000 miles, I griped about what I didn't get: "Thank You for the car, even though it doesn't have a trunk light." In response to a generous gift to the agency where I work, I'd written, "The money will help, but they could have given twice as much."

Something was wrong with those entries because something was wrong with my relationship with God. During the difficult times, it was easy to recognize God's blessings and give praise. But as my life became more stable, I'd begun taking His loving care for granted.

My recent entries are more honest. Yes, I still grumble and complain. But day by day, God is helping me develop the thing that was missing in my previous prayers and in my life—a thankful heart.

Lord, let me honor You with the praise that comes from a truly grateful heart.
—PENNEY SCHWAB

TODAY'S DATE: January 1, 2019

New years Day. I stayed up late last night so stayed in bed til 9 AM. I got up and showered and had breakfast. Read my Bible and prayed over my prayer list. Went to the VFW for the get-together at 3:00. It was for Volunteers and employees of the VFW. There was food and games. There were 4 of us from Monday Music there — Kenny Hurlbut, Donny Mayo, Gai Paul, and myself. We had a good time. It was pretty cold when I left there, −12 I think. Matt went over to Micah & Erik's. It's hard to believe it's 2019. Del has been gone for 3½ years now. It will be 10 years April 25th since Richard passed away. Thank you dear Jesus for helping me every day. Matt lives with me and has since the end of October 2015.

God, may I be inspired to pray more often, over big matters and small,
so that I may become closer to You.

—LINDA NEUKRUG

Then, opening their treasure chests, they offered him gifts of gold, frankincense, and myrrh.

—MATTHEW 2:11 (NRSV)

TODAY'S DATE: _____

Jesus, let me be always ready to give You the gift of myself: my heart, my mind, my body, my actions, my prayers, my faith, my love.

—MARCI ALBORGHETTI

Behold, the heaven and the heaven of heavens is the Lord's thy God,
the earth also, with all that therein is.

—DEUTERONOMY 10:14

TODAY'S DATE: _____

*Lord, how vast is this universe that You have made, and how wonderful beyond all telling that
You should have dwelt as one of us on our small green and blue planet!*

—ANDREW ATTAWAY

Yet those who wait for the Lord . . . will mount up with wings like eagles. . . .

—ISAIAH 40:31 (NAS)

TODAY'S DATE: _____

Jesus, Your name Emmanuel—"God with us"—literally fills me with wonder.

—CAROL KNAPP

Forgetting what is behind and straining toward what is ahead, I press on toward the goal to win the prize for which God has called me heavenward in Christ Jesus.

—PHILIPPIANS 3:13–14 (NIV)

TODAY'S DATE: _____

When my soul is weary and my faith tends to falter, I hear Your voice, Lord, saying, "Press on, press on!"

—FAY ANGUS

He hath put a new song in my mouth, even praise unto our God. . . .

—PSALM 40:3

TODAY'S DATE: _____

_____

_____

_____

_____

_____

_____

_____

_____

_____

_____

_____

_____

_____

_____

_____

_____

_____

_____

Father, a positive attitude is one of the greatest spiritual gifts.
Help me to remember: Praise! Praise! Praise!

—EDWARD GRINNAN

The hearing ear and the seeing eye, the Lord has made them both.

—PROVERBS 20:12 (RSV)

TODAY'S DATE: _____

Lord, I ask politely for the kind of eyesight that sees the glory of the muddy road.

—BRIAN DOYLE

He hath filled the hungry with good things . . . .

—LUKE 1:53

TODAY'S DATE: _____

Lord, train my heart to love what interests You.

—JULIA ATTAWAY

Now return to the Lord your God, For He is gracious and compassionate, slow to anger, abounding in lovingkindness and relenting of evil.

—JOEL 2:13 (NAS)

TODAY'S DATE: _____

Father, You alone are my safe haven, my hope, my peace, my salvation.

—JULIE GARMON

Love each other with brotherly affection and take delight in honoring each other.

—ROMANS 12:10 (TLB)

TODAY'S DATE: _____

Father God, help me to live my life in such a way that people will see my faith in the love I show others.

—DEBBIE MACOMBER

All the days ordained for me were written in your book before one of them came to be.

—PSALM 139:16 (NIV)

TODAY'S DATE: _____

Help me put anxiety aside, Father, and watch Your brush at work on the finished portrait of me.

—ELIZABETH SHERRILL

He guides me along right paths. . . .

—PSALM 23:3 (NLT)

Dear God, help me to trust You wherever I wander.

—MARY ANN O'ROARK

Then He arose and rebuked the wind, and said to the sea, "Peace, be still!" . . .

—MARK 4:39 (NKJV)

TODAY'S DATE: _____

Father, the sea is big and my boat is small, but I feel safe because You are here in the boat with me.

—DANIEL SCHANTZ

For I am the Lord, I change not. . . .

—MALACHI 3:6

In all the changes ahead, Father, keep my eyes fixed on Your unchanging love.

—JOHN SHERRILL

For where your treasure is, there will your heart be also.

—MATTHEW 6:21

I'm curled up in the big old chair by the fireplace in the cabin next door to our house, with my notebook on my lap. It's my time to be alone with God for a day, so I've come to this place made sacred by years of prayers.

It will be a day of gratitude for the richness in my life—my beloved husband Robert, my children, grandchildren and now four new little great-grandchildren; my longtime friends in Nebraska and the newer ones in Colorado; for the many caring readers who write me letters of encouragement, as well as those who are appreciative but don't write. I thank God for the ponderosa pine that seems to bow to me as I look out the front window; the blue spruce I watched my grandfather plant in the 1930s that now towers over the house; for the crispness of morning and the cool night breeze, for potatoes and milk and carrots and cheese; for shimmering aspens that wave to me, and the creek across the road that is God's music; for the living art of white clouds changing form against a lucid blue sky; for. . . .

As I continue my list of treasures, the words stop. I find myself in wordless prayerfulness that will be with me throughout the day as I write in my journal, do a bit of dusting, fix and eat lunch, and just rest in the silence and love of God.

I invite you to find twenty or thirty minutes sometime before the sun sets on this day to sit in a quiet place, kick off your shoes and your cares, and join me in gratitude in companionship with our special friend Jesus. I'll meet you there!

Holy Friend, we've come here to thank You for _____.
(FILL IN THE BLANK)

—MARILYN MORGAN KING

Our Father. . . . Give us this day our daily bread.
—MATTHEW 6:9, 11

I was learning to start every prayer by worshiping God, following the model of the Lord's Prayer, when I noticed something else about this verse. I had seen that not till halfway through the prayer was I allowed to bring up my own concerns. And which concerns, in this model prayer, was I told to focus on? The needs of this day alone. "Pray," Jesus says, "about the chores and choices of the next twenty-four hours only."

What about long-term issues? I thought.

I remembered an Ann Landers column about reader mail. In the ten thousand letters sent her each month, she wrote, a single question appeared most often: What if? "What if I lose my job?" "What if a loved one dies?" Illness, crime, even asteroid collisions—her mail overflowed with fearful possibilities.

I remembered how superior I'd felt to these anxious souls. It's silly to waste energy on things that might never happen! My worries are real ones! Or were they, I wondered now. I glanced back through my prayer journal at the problems that had gobbled time, energy, sleep. And every one of them was firmly rooted in the future.

The whole of the Lord's Prayer has become more meaningful as I direct it toward the next few hours. "Hallowed be thy name in my life this day." "Thy will be done in my life and in the lives of those I'm praying for this day." "Forgive me my trespasses this day." Some of this day's legitimate concerns, of course, may involve preparing for the future, even the distant future—but in day-sized chunks, in quantities I can handle. God alone, the words "this day" tell me, can handle the days to come, held in His safekeeping till they do.

A *Daily Guideposts* reader recently sent me a prayer of St. Augustine that I've made my own:

Our Father, keep me from stain of sin, love me, guide me, lead me, just for today.
—ELIZABETH SHERRILL

I am a traveler passing through the earth, as all my fathers were.

—PSALM 39:12 (TLB)

TODAY'S DATE: _____

Whether I'm going halfway around the world or just down the street, help me, Lord,
to make the most of the journey.

—PENNEY SCHWAB

The heavens are telling the glory of God; they are a marvelous display of his craftsmanship.

—PSALM 19:1 (TLB)

TODAY'S DATE: _____

Father, for the heavenly gifts of nature that You provide, I thank You.

—PATRICIA LORENZ

"You're blessed when you care. At the moment of being 'carefull,' you find yourselves cared for."

—MATTHEW 5:7 (MSG)

TODAY'S DATE: _____

Lord, when I make my days full of simple caring, I really do feel cared for.
Thank You for the blessing.

—KEITH MILLER

"If any want to become my followers, let them deny themselves and take up their cross daily and follow me."

—LUKE 9:23 (NRSV)

TODAY'S DATE: _____

_____

_____

_____

_____

_____

_____

_____

_____

_____

_____

_____

_____

_____

_____

_____

_____

_____

_____

_____

_____

_____

_____

Give me the courage, the strength, the focus, O God, to learn about You and live for You every single day.

—JEFF JAPINGA

Now choose life, so that you and your children may live and that you may love the Lord your God,
listen to his voice, and hold fast to him. For the Lord is your life. . . .

—DEUTERONOMY 30:19—20 (NIV)

TODAY'S DATE: _____

Father, thank You for the Voice that assures me of Your constant love.

—HAROLD HOSTETLER

O Lord, truly I am your servant. . . .

—PSALM 116:16 (NIV)

TODAY'S DATE: _____

Dear Lord, help me work faithfully for You in everything that I do today.

—KAREN BARBER

Fear thou not, for I am with thee. . . .

—ISAIAH 41:10

TODAY'S DATE: _____

Lord, it's when I'm thrown back on myself that I find my need for You.

—BROCK KIDD

Why art thou cast down, O my soul? and why art thou disquieted within me? hope thou in God:
for I shall yet praise him, who is the health of my countenance, and my God.

—PSALM 42:11

TODAY'S DATE: _____

Lord, thank You for the little signs of hope all around me.

—ANDREW ATTAWAY

Now your attitudes and thoughts must all be constantly changing for the better.

—EPHESIANS 4:23 (TLB)

TODAY'S DATE: _____

Lord, open my eyes to the needs of others and show me how I can make a difference today and all year round.

—DEBBIE MACOMBER

A man's mind plans his way, but the Lord directs his steps.

—PROVERBS 16:9 (RSV)

TODAY'S DATE: _____

Holy Spirit, please help me to remember that if something isn't working,
with God's help, I can change things.

—MARY ANN O'ROARK

But lay up for yourselves treasures in heaven . . .
For where your treasure is, there will your heart be also.

—MATTHEW 6:20–21

TODAY'S DATE: _____

Lord, when I've fixed my mind on earthly treasures, help me to lift up my eyes and look to You.

—JEFF CHU

Thou shalt love thy neighbour as thyself. . . .

—MARK 12:31

TODAY'S DATE: _____

Help me to think of my neighbor first, Father, in all I do today.

—ELIZABETH SHERRILL

Thou shalt guide me. . . .

—PSALM 73:24

TODAY'S DATE: _____

Father, be present with us, our steady Guide, pointing out the way You want us to go.

—PAM KIDD

You faithfully answer our prayers with awesome deeds, O God our savior . . . .

—PSALM 65:5 (NLT)

TODAY'S DATE: _____

You are awesome, God! Thank You for answering our prayers.

—PABLO DIAZ

What man is he that desireth life, and loveth many days, that he may see good?
—PSALM 34:12

A statue honoring Anne Frank, the Dutch teenager whose World War II diary won her worldwide fame, was unveiled in 1977 in Amsterdam near the canal house where she and her Jewish family took refuge with sympathetic Christians. After two years of hiding, the Otto Frank family was discovered, captured and imprisoned by the Nazis. Anne died in 1945 in the Belsen concentration camp at the age of fifteen.

Some years ago I recall visiting the house where the Franks hid out and reading photostatic copies of pages taken from the sensitive and courageous girl's diary. Of all the things she wrote, nothing has stayed with me as much as this line: "In spite of everything, I think people are really good at heart."

That's quite a testimony of faith when one considers the circumstance in which it was written. But it is full of insight. When you begin to think the opposite—that most everyone is inconsiderate, uncaring, unloving, materialistic, self-serving—look again, closer. All about you are people who give of their time, talent and financial resources without thought of return—rescue squad workers, volunteer firefighters, church workers, social service aides, Girl Scout and Boy Scout leaders, Little League coaches, school and hospital volunteers. Their treasure is not vulnerable to moth and rust and thieves (Matthew 6:20), and neither will yours if you do likewise.

There is much to be positive about, Lord. Help me see life's bright side.
—FRED BAUER

Come now, and let us reason together, saith the Lord. . . .
—ISAIAH 1:18

"Can we take the ferry?" my daughter Maria asked, as she does every summer when we visit Coronado, California. The ferry crosses San Diego Bay from Coronado to the city's harbor, a fifteen-minute ride.

"Why, what do you want to do when we get over there?" I asked. She shrugged.

"I don't care about being there," she said. "I just want to go there." Sounds like something Yogi Berra might say, but it makes sense. Everybody knows the best part is the traveling.

I've been keeping a prayer journal for the last few months, and I'm learning that prayer is like that. I've been praying for a friend to forgive me, and I've been disappointed because I haven't seen the desired result. But as I write my concerns and the nudges from God I feel in return, I learn that prayer is more a conversation than a list of demands. In talking to God about my friend's forgiveness, I've learned a lot about myself. I've discovered I can be a better friend by being more understanding and watching what I say more carefully. As I listen in prayer, I'm also getting to know God better and learning what He wants for my life.

When I review my prayer journal, I see that not all my prayers have been answered yet. But what may be more important is what's happened to me through the asking. My growth is a reminder that prayer is like that ferry ride. As my young daughter well knew, it's not the "being there" that matters, it's the "getting there."

God in heaven, hear my prayers and lead me on a never-ending journey to know You better.
—GINA BRIDGEMAN

Who can understand his errors? cleanse thou me from secret faults.

—PSALM 19:12

TODAY'S DATE: _____

Forgive me for all my faults, Lord. You more than anyone know what they are.

—RICK HAMLIN

So then, as we have opportunity, let us do good to all. . . .

—GALATIANS 6:10 (RSV)

TODAY'S DATE: _____

Dear God, reveal to me a selfless act that I can do today.

—KAREN VALENTIN

Now be strong . . . for I am with you, saith the Lord of hosts.

—HAGGAI 2:4

TODAY'S DATE: _____

Lord, help me to remember that underneath all my fears, You are there to be my strength.

—BROCK KIDD

For in him we live, and move, and have our being. . . .

—ACTS 17:28

TODAY'S DATE: _____

Empowered by You, Lord, I face the future unafraid.

—MARY LOU CARNEY

Bless the Lord, O my soul, And forget none of His benefits.

—PSALM 103:2 (NAS)

TODAY'S DATE: _____

Thank You, Lord, for multiplying the efforts we make on Your behalf.

—ALMA BARKMAN

Lord, you have been our dwelling place throughout all generations. Before the mountains were born or you brought forth the earth and the world, from everlasting to everlasting you are God.

—PSALM 90:1–2 (NIV)

TODAY'S DATE: _____

Lord God, You Who are the Alpha and the Omega, the Beginning and the End,
help me to stay with you in the here and now.

—SHARI SMYTH

The Lord is your keeper....

—PSALM 121:5 (NKJV)

TODAY'S DATE: _____

_____

_____

_____

_____

_____

_____

_____

_____

_____

_____

_____

_____

_____

_____

_____

_____

_____

_____

_____

_____

_____

Dear Lord, help me to remember that sometimes as much as I want to help,
my efforts are best spent putting my trust in You.

—SABRA CIANCANELLI

"The Lord will guide you always; he will satisfy your needs in a sun-scorched land and will strengthen your frame. You will be like a well-watered garden, like a spring whose waters never fail."

—ISAIAH 58:11 (NIV)

TODAY'S DATE: _____

Thank You, Father, for using our suffering to grow our love and empathy for others.

—HELEN GRACE LESCHEID

"The one who trusts in him will never be put to shame."

—ROMANS 9:33 (NIV)

TODAY'S DATE: _____

Lord, help me to strive to trust You more.

—DOLPHUS WEARY

I will praise thee, O Lord my God, with all my heart: and I will glorify thy name for evermore.

—PSALM 86:12

TODAY'S DATE: _____

Lord, day by day, help me to do what You have designed me to do.

—JEFF CHU

He maketh me to lie down in green pastures: he leadeth me beside the still waters.

He restoreth my soul. . . .

—PSALM 23:2–3

TODAY'S DATE: _____

Father, restore my soul through deep and abiding rest.

—SCOTT WALKER

When he calls to me, I will answer him. . . .

—PSALM 91:15 (RSV)

TODAY'S DATE: _____

Let me feel Your nearness, Father, as I pray.

—ELIZABETH SHERRILL

"And lo, I am with you always, even to the end of the age."

—MATTHEW 28:20 (NAS)

TODAY'S DATE: _____

Jesus, thank You for being beside me all these years. Help me love You more, always more.

—JULIA ATTAWAY

*"Whoever believes in me, as the Scripture has said, streams of
living water will flow from within him."*

—JOHN 7:38 (NIV)

TODAY'S DATE: _____

Lord, in Your mercy, even my tears can become the water of life.

—BROCK KIDD

Teach us to number our days, that we may apply our hearts unto wisdom.
—PSALM 90:12

*H*ave you ever played this conversational game with friends: "If I knew I had only a year to live, what changes would I make in my life?" I'm glad I've had some practice in considering that question, because it's recently become a very real issue for me.

I'm feeling in excellent health just now, and for that I'm very grateful. But the reality of my particular variety of cancer is that long-term survival rates are very low. The possibility of a new metastasis popping up on the radar screens of my CT scans forces me to plan my life in very short blocks of time. Booking plane tickets or scheduling visits to faraway family or friends is difficult—I find myself unable to plan anything with much certainty beyond the next scheduled checkup.

One doctor friend suggested that I consider the six weeks until my next scans as a gift box of time, a gift to be opened with care, thoughtfulness and joy. None of us knows just how many days we'll have on this earth. It's so easy to get caught up in the urgencies of everyday life and miss what we know to be the really important things.

Recently I wrote in my journal, "Will I ever wake up in the morning and not appreciate our clean air and blue sky, the fragrance and beauty of the garden in bloom, the joy of [my husband] Harry's faithful loving? Probably. But I hope not. I'd like to be acutely aware of each day."

Maybe a whole year to consider making changes in the way we live is too long. My latest thinking is that every new stage of life (college, job, marriage, parenthood, retirement) should come with these instructions: "For maximum enjoyment, measure out in six-week increments."

O Lord of the moments, accept my thanks as I open the gift box of this day.
—MARY JANE CLARK

"Write in a book all the words that I have spoken to you."

—JEREMIAH 30:2 (RSV)

My husband John thought we'd seen the whales off the coast of California; I was sure we'd seen them from Maui. He said we'd gone to Canada before the year we spent in Bolivia; I thought it was after we got back. And that shoebox full of photos! Was this slate-roofed house in Austria or Switzerland? And what were the names of this couple who'd been so kind to us when our car broke down?

After years of such unsolvable mysteries, I'd finally begun to keep a travel diary, a separate notebook for each trip, small pages so it wouldn't become a chore. It was still an effort some nights, after a day on the move, to get the notebook out and record the highlights.

But the rewards! I have forty years of trip logs now, and opening any one of them at random brings back people, places, small crises, discoveries and surprise encounters—most of which I'd forgotten.

Shortly after I began taking notes on trips, I started a spiritual diary. I jotted down quotes, poems, insights, questions, prayers, confessions, words I believed I was hearing from God—always with a date, place and shorthand summary of the situation.

And like the external events in the travel diaries that would otherwise be forgotten, these inner episodes come as revelations when I read them now. I had no idea how many prayers had been answered until I read entry after entry and marveled at outcomes I could never have foreseen. I had no idea how truly a journey this Christian walk is until I could trace mine over time. Not, alas, ever upward and onward. Like any journey, this one is beset with detours and setbacks and disappointments. But full, too, of sudden glorious vistas, and always with fresh glimpses of Him Who is both the goal and the way.

Lord of the journey, what notes will I make today on the trip whose destination only You can see?

—ELIZABETH SHERRILL

The Sovereign Lord is my strength; he makes my feet like the feet of a deer,

he enables me to go on the heights. . . .

—HABAKKUK 3:19 (NIV)

TODAY'S DATE: _____

Lord, help me to continue to learn how to depend on You, and help me to offer everything to You, including my pride.

—DOLPHUS WEARY

Lord, I believe; help thou mine unbelief.

—MARK 9:24

TODAY'S DATE: _____

Dear Lord, help me to remember that when I feed my fears, I lose sight of my connection to You.

—SABRA CIANCANELLI

Trust in the Lord with all your heart and do not lean on your own understanding.

—PROVERBS 3:5 (NAS)

TODAY'S DATE: _____

Help me to trust You in all things, Lord, and to leave the results to You.

—ROBERTA MESSNER

Give me understanding according to thy word.

—PSALM 119:169

TODAY'S DATE: _____

Lord, my words so often fail, but Your Word never does, in or out of season.

—MARK COLLINS

Sing unto the Lord a new song. . . .

—PSALM 98:1

TODAY'S DATE: _____

Father, we sing the praises of those very special people who never quit saying yes to life. Let me be a hero like them.

—PAM KIDD

God Almighty . . . will bless you with blessings of heaven above,
blessings of the deep that couches beneath. . . .

—GENESIS 49:25 (RSV)

TODAY'S DATE: _____

Open my eyes, Lord, to Your abundance. Amen.

—KAREN VALENTIN

Every good and perfect gift is from above, coming down from the Father. . . .

—JAMES 1:17 (NIV)

TODAY'S DATE: _____

Even in little things, Father, may I see opportunity for beauty and service.

—MARY LOU CARNEY

"Surely the Lord is in this place. . . ."

—GENESIS 28:16 (NIV)

TODAY'S DATE: _____

Lord, somehow You always remind us that You are near.

—CAROL KUYKENDALL

Open thou mine eyes, that I may behold wondrous things out of thy law.

—PSALM 119:18

TODAY'S DATE: _____

Dear Lord, Unimaginable One, Giver of Everything That Is, thank You.
There are no small things, are there, Father? Only eyes too closed to see.

—BRIAN DOYLE

When I am afraid, I will trust in You.

—PSALM 56:3 (NIV)

TODAY'S DATE: _____

Thank You, God, for the special times You make Yourself known in my loneliness.
—LINDA NEUKRUG

"I will not leave you desolate; I will come to you."

—JOHN 14:18 (RSV)

TODAY'S DATE: _____

Lord, thank You for sending the Light to guide us all the way home to You.

—KEITH MILLER

Let the fields rejoice, and all that is therein.

—I CHRONICLES 16:32

TODAY'S DATE: _____

Lord, teach me to rejoice in all Your gifts in every season of the year.

—PHILIP ZALESKI

This I recall to my mind, therefore have I hope. It is of the Lord's mercies that we are not consumed, because his compassions fail not. They are new every morning: great is thy faithfulness.

—LAMENTATIONS 3:21–23

TODAY'S DATE: _____

Lord, thank You for all living creatures that awaken me to Your faithfulness in never failing to bring a new day and the hope that comes with it.

—SHARI SMYTH

The fruit of the Spirit is love, joy, peace, patience, kindness, goodness, faithfulness.

—GALATIANS 5:22 (NIV)

TODAY'S DATE: _____

Lord, may I grow more like You each and every day.

—DEBBIE MACOMBER

And there I will meet with thee, and I will commune with thee from above the mercy seat....
—EXODUS 25:22

My son Jon, his twin brother Jeremy, his sisters Julie and Jennifer, his stepfather Gene and I were crowded together in Room 48 of the small motel at Dunklin Memorial Camp in Florida—a city of refuge where men like Jon are set free from all kinds of addictions. We all knew that Jon was learning how to communicate effectively with God, and today he shared his prayer journal with us.

"Father, thank You for getting them all here safely. Thank You for hearing my prayers, and being attentive to my heart and to my family's hearts this morning. Thank You also for knowing exactly how to work in each of their lives and for preparing a place in eternity for each of us. Father, speak to me about the worry I had yesterday and about my forgetting You."

"They all see a little more of My Son in you. Know that your struggles have purpose, and trust that I am capable. My spirit, the Spirit of Jehovah, lives in you. Now you cannot forget for long that you are Mine and that I shape every detail of your life. I want you to know that you are accepting responsibility for your actions. There is no one to blame but yourself for your chemical addiction, and I have taken the blame and thrown it away. I cannot even see your sin. All I see is that you are My son for eternity. How can anything I have chosen run from Me? I gave it the ability to run and the will to run. Surely I can call it back. I hear every prayer from your family and anoint the answer with My testimony."

We all wept openly together. We had never been so close as a family.

Holy Father, starting today, teach me to commune with You through prayer and journaling as my son does.

—MARION BOND WEST

Fix your thoughts on what is true and good and right. . . .
—PHILIPPIANS 4:8 (TLB)

When I heard that a former colleague had said something untrue about me, I exploded. I corrected the misinformation and ticked off a list of the woman's offenses, growing angrier with each word. At about number seven, I paused for breath. It was then I remembered that my Aunt Annie kept a list too: a Goodness File. Instead of dwelling on hurts, she chose to record the spirit-lifters she received through the years.

Her file began in April 1962 when she was sent to interview University of Oklahoma football coach Bud Wilkinson. She was so nervous, she dropped her purse as she entered his office and watched in horror as the contents rolled under Wilkinson's desk. Without saying a word, he crawled under it, retrieved everything and brushed off her apologies.

"How good of you to come!" he said warmly. He then answered her questions fully and thoughtfully.

Aunt Annie recorded dozens of other incidents. She received a gift of pink peonies from a student who never spoke in class. An exhausted construction worker, coming off the night shift, gave her his seat on a crowded bus. "You have a full workday ahead of you, while I'm going home to rest," he said. A postal clerk searched the lobby and even the sidewalk to find her missing earring.

I've started a Goodness File, too, and discovered that when I concentrate on people's good points, their faults become much less irritating.

Help me to look for goodness, Lord, and to recognize it in everyone I meet.
—PENNEY SCHWAB

Heal me, O Lord, and I shall be healed; save me, and I shall be saved. . . .

—JEREMIAH 17:14

TODAY'S DATE: _____

God, You have so many ways of giving me Your healing touch.

—RICK HAMLIN

"Do not be afraid, little flock, for it is your Father's good pleasure to give you the kingdom."

—LUKE 12:32 (NRSV)

TODAY'S DATE: _____

Father, let me seek You as eagerly as I seek those here on earth who love me.

—MARCI ALBORGHETTI

Do not withhold your mercy from me, O Lord; may your love and your truth always protect me.

—PSALM 40:11 (NIV)

TODAY'S DATE: _____

Thank You, Father, for understanding who we are and choosing to accept our childlike faith.

—DOLPHUS WEARY

Oh that men would praise the Lord for his goodness. . . .

—PSALM 107:15

TODAY'S DATE: _____

Father, even the scars I carry in life are reasons to sing Your praises.

—BROCK KIDD

As you learn more and more how God works, you will learn how to do your work.

—COLOSSIANS 1:10 (MSG)

TODAY'S DATE: _____

Lord, thank You for Your Word and for the people
all around us from whom we can learn Your will.

—KEITH MILLER

For you did not receive a spirit that makes you a slave again to fear....

—ROMANS 8:15 (NIV)

TODAY'S DATE: _____

Teach me, Father, to distinguish needful fears from the false ones
that block full enjoyment of Your world.

—ELIZABETH SHERRILL

We give thanks to you, O God. . . .

—PSALM 75:1 (NIV)

TODAY'S DATE: _____

God, please give me the perspective to see the blessings You've provided me.

—JOSHUA SUNDQUIST

O taste and see that the Lord is good. . . .

—PSALM 34:8

TODAY'S DATE: _____

Help me, Father, to treasure the many ways You've given us to experience Your limitless creation!

—JOHN SHERRILL

Am I now trying to win the approval of men, or of God? . . .

—GALATIANS 1:10 (NIV)

TODAY'S DATE: _____

Dear Lord, help me to do what pleases You and not worry about what others think.

—KAREN BARBER

I am the light of the world: he that followeth me shall not walk in darkness,
but shall have the light of life.

—JOHN 8:12

TODAY'S DATE: _____

Oh, Christ, the true light Who enlightens and sanctifies us, let the light of Your countenance be impressed upon us, that in it we may see Your unapproachable light.

—MARY BROWN

They will be called oaks of righteousness, a planting of the Lord for the display of his splendor.

—ISAIAH 61:3 (NIV)

TODAY'S DATE: _____

Father, help me always to do my best and to concentrate on the things that will last.

—HAROLD HOSTETLER

Then the Lord opened the servant's eyes, and he looked and saw. . . .

—II KINGS 6:17 (NIV)

TODAY'S DATE: _____

Father, I'm so grateful that even my mistakes can be lessons learned. Today, please show me how to bring my earthly perspective in line with Your heavenly one.

—KAREN BARBER

Even the night shall be light about me.

—PSALM 139:11 (NKJV)

TODAY'S DATE: _____

Forgive me, Lord, for fearing the dark. I should have known You would be there too.

—DANIEL SCHANTZ

I long to . . . take refuge in the shelter of your wings.

—PSALM 61:4 (NIV)

I'm leaning, leaning, leaning on Your everlasting arms, Lord!

—MARY LOU CARNEY

This is the day which the Lord hath made; we will rejoice and be glad in it.

—PSALM 118:24

Many years ago, while visiting my grandparents, I found an old copy of *Daily Guideposts* that belonged to my grandmother and read a few pages. The daily devotionals were inspiring, but it was the daily journal sections at the end of each month that really caught my attention.

My grandmother had written some type of praise to God each day, thanking Him for the many blessings He had provided for them. What was so amazing to me was that her thanks and praise continued all during the time my grandfather's only sister was dying. I was much younger then and it took many more years for me to incorporate daily praise to God in all things.

Today, I begin each journal entry with TYFT—Thank You for Today—no matter what happened that day. I don't have the time to write as extensively as I would like, but the Daily Guideposts journal makes it possible for me to express in writing my daily thanks to God.

Thank You, God, for this day and that I can use it to watch for
all your blessings and write them down.

—SHARON HOWARD

"Follow me," Jesus told him, and Levi got up and followed him.
—MARK 2:14 (NIV)

I used to wonder how Jesus could have had such an impact on the lives of His disciples in the few years He spent with them. But that was before I met Bill, the pastor of the church I attend at college. Young men from my college have been attending Bill's Friday afternoon Bible study for more than two decades—longer than I've been alive. When I came to the Bible study, I was full of doubts and worries. One Friday afternoon, I talked about my struggles, half expecting a stern reprimand from Bill.

"What's the opposite of faith?" Bill asked.

"Doubt," someone said.

"No," said Bill. "The Bible tells us to walk by faith and not by sight, remember? The opposite of faith is sight. Doubt is just a natural part of growing in your faith."

I wrote down those words in a journal in which I've written hundreds of other things that Bill has taught me over these past few years. And it's not just me. On his birthday, at homecoming and during other times throughout the year, men ranging in age from their early twenties to almost forty can be found in Bill's living room, spending time with the man who helped their faith grow roots.

Jesus had a great impact on His disciples. As Bill has shown me, all it takes is the willingness to share your life and your love—and your Friday afternoons.

Lord, thank You for the mentors who have helped me along my spiritual journey.
—JOSHUA SUNDQUIST

I have not run in vain, neither laboured in vain.

—PHILIPPIANS 2:16

TODAY'S DATE: _____

What a precious gift life is, Lord. Help me savor every minute of it and every mile.

—RICK HAMLIN

For every one that exalteth himself shall be abased; and he that humbleth himself shall be exalted.

—LUKE 18:14

TODAY'S DATE: _____

Father, we come as we are and thank You for being good.

—PAM KIDD

Thou shalt not be afraid for the terror by night; nor for the arrow that flieth by day; Nor for the pestilence that walketh in darkness; nor for the destruction that wasteth at noonday.

—PSALM 91:5–6

TODAY'S DATE: _____

Lord, You came into this world and walked among the sick, never fearing.
Grant me protection, but also grant me Your compassion.

—EDWARD GRINNAN

For with God nothing shall be impossible.

—LUKE 1:37

Let me look beyond limitations of time and space, Father, to the vastness of life in You.

—ELIZABETH SHERRILL

He hath made every thing beautiful in his time. . . .

—ECCLESIASTES 3:11

TODAY'S DATE: _____

Lord, teach me to see the beauty in every corner of Your kingdom.

—PHILIP ZALESKI

"You are the light of the world. A city built on a hill cannot be hid."

—MATTHEW 5:14 (NRSV)

TODAY'S DATE: _____

Lord, let me see the light of Your hope everywhere I look.

—MARCI ALBORGHETTI

If one falls down, his friend can help him up. . . .

—ECCLESIASTES 4:10 (NIV)

TODAY'S DATE: _____

God, thank You for the friends You give me.

—PABLO DIAZ

Aspire to lead a quiet life, to mind your own business, and to work with your own hands. . . .

—I THESSALONIANS 4:II (NKJV)

TODAY'S DATE: _____

Lord, draw me today to some project that I can complete as a working prayer.

—EVELYN BENCE

Then God said, "Let the waters teem with fish and other life,
and let the skies be filled with birds of every kind."

—GENESIS 1:20 (TLB)

TODAY'S DATE: _____

Praise the Lord from the heavens, praise Him from the skies. The sun by day, the moon by night,
drifting clouds and birds that fly, Your glory fills the earth, O God of all creation!

—FAY ANGUS

The fear of the Lord is the beginning of wisdom. . . .

—PSALM III:IO

TODAY'S DATE: _____

Dear Lord, the beginning of wisdom rests in You and is therefore ours for all eternity.
—BRENDA WILBEE

The cheerful heart has a continual feast.

—PROVERBS 15:15 (NIV)

TODAY'S DATE: _____

God, remind me that I don't have to be in a helping profession to help someone. In any job—or none—I can be a helper and a healer.

—LINDA NEUKRUG

"I am the true vine, and my Father is the vine dresser. . . . I am the vine, you are the branches.
He who abides in Me, and I in him, bears much fruit; for without Me you can do nothing."

—JOHN 15:1, 5 (NKJV)

TODAY'S DATE: _____

_____

_____

_____

_____

_____

_____

_____

_____

_____

_____

_____

_____

_____

_____

_____

_____

_____

Dear God, what a precious gift You've given me, to be a branch in Your beloved vineyard. Please help me remember, especially during trials and struggles, that You are holding on to me.

—MARY BROWN

"In his hand is the life of every creature and the breath of all mankind."

—JOB 12:10 (NIV)

TODAY'S DATE: _____

*Dear God, help me always to be grateful for the gift of being alive,
and use it to bring light and life wherever I go.*

—ANNE ADRIANCE

What does the Lord require of you but to do justice, to love kindness,
and to walk humbly with your God?

—MICAH 6:8 (NAS)

TODAY'S DATE: _____

Father, give me the courage to follow my gladness and joy in the service of others.

—SCOTT WALKER

"Let your hand be with me, and keep me from harm so that I will be free from pain. . . ."
—I CHRONICLES 4:IO (NIV)

This year, my birthday fell on a regular workday, so I took the day off, just as I've done for the last several years. "Why?" asked a co-worker who is many years younger. "When you become an adult, isn't your birthday just like any other day?"

"Actually, I have this thing about birthdays," I told her. "I see them as God's gift of a once-a-year day to celebrate the person He's created each of us to be, and an opportunity to pause and consider where we are in the process of becoming that person."

She rolled her eyes, so I continued to defend my birthday theory. "It's a day when you're supposed to have a private birthday party with God."

"How?" she asked.

"I like to find a nice quiet place outside. Sometimes it's at the table on our back patio, or on top of a rock by a stream in the mountains, or on a bench in the shade at a nearby park. I take a notebook and my Bible. I read and reflect back and look forward and talk to God and listen to Him, asking Him where we are in my growing-up process. I always end by writing a birthday prayer, filled with 'thank-you's for past blessings and 'pleases' for future ones. Then I tuck the prayer in my journal or Bible so I can read it several times during the year. Later in the day, I like to celebrate with my family and friends."

She gave me one more roll of her eyes before turning and walking away, as if my birthday tradition sounded a bit odd to her. But when her birthday fell on a regular workday a few weeks later, she took the day off, too.

Father, thank You for my once-a-year birthday and the opportunity to celebrate with You.
—CAROL KUYKENDALL

"He who brings thanksgiving as his sacrifice honors me. . . ."

—PSALM 50:23 (RSV)

Kathy's been coming in for kidney dialysis for thirteen years, always with a smile and a warm "How do you do?" One evening I asked her how she maintained her buoyant attitude.

"I keep a grateful journal! Every day I write down five things I'm grateful for."

"What kinds of things?"

"Oh, like the sun coming out." In the Pacific Northwest this is unusual and merits attention! "Or like the man who let me merge in front of him," she went on, "when I was getting on the freeway tonight. You'd be surprised how finding just five things a day changes your whole outlook."

I decided to try it. Pretty soon I noticed that I was recording conversations I had with people, sometimes complete strangers who took time out of their day to be pleasant: the carpenter dressed in overalls who poured my coffee in the convenience store; the old widower at the sauna who detected I was a Canadian; a store clerk who remembered I ski and asked about this year's snow.

It didn't take long to realize Kathy was right—but not in the way I'd expected. True, the very act of looking for daily blessings did encourage me to see things that had gone unnoticed before. But more importantly, I discovered myself recreating these little "people moments" for someone else. What made me feel recognized and human, I started passing on. A student's "Nice boots, teach!" became my "Danny, you're looking on top of the world! What's up?"

I still write in my grateful journal, but not for myself anymore. I write because the kindness of other people keeps me supplied with ideas on how to spice up someone else's otherwise unnotable day.

Thank You, Lord, for Kathy's grateful journal. May I increasingly give thanks and be found giving those around me something for which to be grateful.

—BRENDA WILBEE

Thy word is . . . a light to my path.

—PSALM 119:105 (RSV)

TODAY'S DATE: _____

Speak to me today, Father, through Your written Word.

—ELIZABETH SHERRILL

"Love one another. As I have loved you, so you must love one another."

—JOHN 13:34 (NIV)

TODAY'S DATE: _____

Father, thank You for loving me unconditionally. Help me pass that love along today to someone who needs it.

—MARY LOU CARNEY

God loves a cheerful giver.

—II CORINTHIANS 9:7 (NAS)

TODAY'S DATE: _____

With You, Lord, there is always more than enough. Help me to give freely.

—ROBERTA MESSNER

When the wind did not allow us to hold our course, we sailed to the lee of Crete . . .

and came to a place called Fair Havens. . . .

—ACTS 27:7—8 (NIV)

TODAY'S DATE: _____

*Lord, blow us off course from our usual day to day and help us to see and enjoy
the beauty of the fair havens to which You send us.*

—SHARON FOSTER

Praise be to the God and Father of our Lord Jesus Christ, who has blessed us in the heavenly realms with every spiritual blessing in Christ.

—EPHESIANS 1:3 (NIV)

TODAY'S DATE: _____

Keep me from being so downcast, Lord, that I forget to look for the flowers lining my pathway.

—MARY LOU CARNEY

Though thy beginning was small, yet thy latter end should greatly increase.

—JOB 8:7

TODAY'S DATE: _____

Show me, Father, where in my life You want me to take that one small step.

I will trust, and not be afraid. . . .

—ISAIAH 12:2

TODAY'S DATE: _____

Grant me the courage, Lord, to greet the world rather than run from it.

—PHILIP ZALESKI

And walk in love, as Christ also hath loved us. . . .

—EPHESIANS 5:2

TODAY'S DATE: _____

Lord, thank You for loving me even in my weaknesses.

—JULIA ATTAWAY

"See, I am doing a new thing! Now it springs up; do you not perceive it? . . . "

—ISAIAH 43:19 (NIV)

TODAY'S DATE: _____

Dear God, help me to give up my frenzied over planning and enjoy each day as it unfolds.

—MARY ANN O'ROARK

Let us lift up our heart . . . unto God. . . .

—LAMENTATIONS 3:41

TODAY'S DATE: _____

Lord, today may I play my role in dealing with the troubles before me—
may I open myself to You so that You can do the lifting.

—JOHN SHERRILL

Having gifts that differ according to the grace given to us, let us use them. . . .

—ROMANS 12:6 (RSV)

TODAY'S DATE: _____

Dear Lord, You've given all of us our own talents and abilities, and when we share them,
we do for each other what we were meant to do.

—ANNE ADRIANCE

"Come, all you who are thirsty. . . . Come, buy wine and milk without money and without cost. Why spend money on what is not bread, and your labor on what does not satisfy? . . ."

—ISAIAH 55:I—2 (NIV)

TODAY'S DATE: _____

Lord Jesus, my Bread of Life, I want You to nourish my soul.
Help me receive You today in every way You offer Yourself.

—MARY BROWN

He will teach us of his ways, and we will walk in his paths. . . .

—MICAH 4:2

TODAY'S DATE: _____

Lord, keep me on the right path, and when I take a wrong turn,
help me to recognize my mistake and go back to You.

—JEFF CHU

So teach us to number our days, that we may apply our hearts unto wisdom.

—PSALM 90:12

TODAY'S DATE: _____

Lord, keep me from seeing my days as something I own but as a gift that comes from You.

—SCOTT WALKER

"I am with you always."

—MATTHEW 28:20 (RSV)

The year was 1990, and I'd just arrived home from a delightful evening of reminiscing, laughter and comradeship. A couple who'd moved away had come back for a visit, so my friends Helen and Bob had invited the old gang over for the evening. It was nice of them to include me, but there was no way to avoid the glaring truth that I was now single—one-half of a couple.

As I walked into my dark and empty house, I felt more alone than ever before, and the chill of the February night went all the way into my bones. At that moment, I looked up to the framed needlepoint cross hanging by my prayer chair. Sewn by a *Daily Guideposts* reader who had sent it to comfort me at this difficult time in my life, it bore the words of Jesus: "I am with you always."

Oh, how desperately I wanted to believe it! But could I honestly claim such a wild, unprovable truth? As the wind howled outside my window, I sank into my prayer chair, closed my eyes and fell into the waiting silence. Then I began to breathe those words into my heart, repeating them silently, letting them fill my empty heart: *I am with you always . . . I am with you always . . . I am . . .*

I continued the practice daily, and as the weeks and months unfolded, I found the words taking up residence in my heart. From this sturdy rock my life began to flow like a trusting river. Without trying to make anything happen, I felt led to reach out to form new friendships, to find spiritual companionship in group prayer and Bible study, and to get to know myself better through keeping a daily journal. There were down days, too, when I was ambushed by loneliness or when a friend's death brought awareness of my own diminishing years. At such moments, those five aligning words would come up unbidden from my heart to remind me I could trust God to bring me through the rockiest of riverbeds.

Knowing You are with me always, Lord, I can trust You to carry me to wholeness.

—MARILYN MORGAN KING

This is the day which the Lord has made; Let us rejoice and be glad in it.
—PSALM 118:24 (NAS)

I was at the bank, standing in line at the teller's window. As the gentleman ahead of me finished up his business, the teller said, "Have a nice day!"

The smiling gentleman, grandson in tow, answered, "I always say, 'Make it a nice day!'"

Make it a nice day! Is it truly in my power to do such a thing? I wondered for the rest of that Monday. *Can I really fashion a day to my liking? Well, at least I can try.*

My process of "making a nice day" began in tiny increments, starting with jotting in my journal just what I thought a nice day would be. It would certainly begin with ample prayer time, so that evening I set my alarm clock for a half hour earlier. And that new vanilla coffee I'd spotted at the supermarket too; I added that to my shopping list. The living room cleaned up before going to bed would surely be nice come morning, so I made a new ritual of counting off ten things that I would put away before retiring. Soon I was having such a good time that I increased it to twenty things. Before a month was out, I was getting a handle on the papers that cluttered my life. And before I knew it, I'd reshaped my life, one choice at a time.

Won't you join me in making this day—this life—a great one?

I give You my life, Lord, one day at a time.
—ROBERTA MESSNER

What shall I render unto the Lord for all his benefits toward me?

—PSALM 116:12

TODAY'S DATE: _____

What I can give, Lord, I give: my heart, my self.

—RICK HAMLIN

The Lord, your God, is in your midst....

—ZEPHANIAH 3:17 (NRSV)

TODAY'S DATE: _____

In those quiet spaces of my life, oh, God, help me to listen for You
instead of filling them with my own noise.

—JEFF JAPINGA

Blessed are the peacemakers: for they shall be called the children of God.

—MATTHEW 5:9

TODAY'S DATE: _____

Father, what is the work of peace You have for me today?

—ELIZABETH SHERRILL

Thanks be to God for his indescribable gift!

—II CORINTHIANS 9:15 (NIV)

TODAY'S DATE: _____

Oh, Jesus, the Father's beloved Son, what a gift You are!

—JULIA ATTAWAY

"Therefore do not be anxious for tomorrow, for tomorrow will be anxious for itself. . . ."
—MATTHEW 6:34 (RSV)

TODAY'S DATE: _____

Father, help me not to be anxious for tomorrow. May I seek first Your kingdom and Your righteousness, and all I need will be provided.

—SCOTT WALKER

So do not throw away your confidence, it will be richly rewarded. You need to persevere so that when you have done the will of God, you will receive what he has promised.

—HEBREWS 10:35–36 (NIV)

TODAY'S DATE: _____

Divine Shepherd, bless each of your children today. Comfort them, guide them and when they get discouraged, carry them in Your arms, close to Your heart.

—HELEN GRACE LESCHEID

Thou art the God that doest wonders. . . .

—PSALM 77:14

TODAY'S DATE: _____

Let me look with fresh eyes, Father, at all I see today.

—ELIZABETH SHERRILL

And on earth peace. . . .

—LUKE 2:14

TODAY'S DATE: _____

Peace, Father, beautiful peace. Amen.

—PAM KIDD

And this is the promise that he hath promised us, even eternal life.

—1 JOHN 2:25

TODAY'S DATE: _____

Dear Lord, well, finally, half a century after You put me on this planet,
I get it that who we really are doesn't die. Thanks.

—BRIAN DOYLE

Glad and merry in heart....

—II CHRONICLES 7:10

TODAY'S DATE: _____

Father! I praise You for Your Son, the greatest Gift ever given.

—MARION BOND WEST

Worship the Lord in the beauty of holiness.

—I CHRONICLES 16:29

TODAY'S DATE: _____

Keep me, Lord, in this front-row seat with the perfect view of Your creation.

—RICK HAMLIN

When life is heavy and hard to take, go off by yourself. Enter the silence. Bow in prayer.

Don't ask questions: Wait for hope to appear. Don't run from trouble.

Take it full-face. The "worst" is never the worst.

—LAMENTATIONS 3:28–30 (MSG)

TODAY'S DATE: _____

You fulfill my every need, Father. May I always turn to You instead of relying on my own resources, no matter what the situation.

—DEBBIE MACOMBER

Give thanks unto the Lord, call upon his name, make known his deeds among the people.

—I CHRONICLES 16:8

TODAY'S DATE: _____

Lord, how can I have gone in such a short time from the depths of heartbreak to a new life of service? Only by Your grace.

—BROCK KIDD

Let no one seek his own good, but the good of his neighbor.

—I CORINTHIANS 10:24 (RSV)

Dear God, just as You are gracious enough to fulfill my needs, thank You
for using me to fulfill a need for someone else this year.
—LINDA NEUKRUG

So I commended enjoyment....
—ECCLESIASTES 8:15 (NKJV)

I've always admired the ability of American GIs to find humor in the dark world of warfare. The TV series *M*A*S*H* illustrated this gift for handling pain with a well-phrased wisecrack or practical prank.

My Uncle John, who lives in Eureka Springs, Arkansas, was a gunner in World War II, stationed in the Philippines and New Guinea, where he served with honor. In his diary, Uncle John recounts some of the lighter moments, like the time his trench-buddy was snoring so loudly that he drew enemy fire.

At Breakneck Ridge, Uncle John had gone without a bath for a month, crawling around in muddy trenches in the same clothes every day. His shoes were lost in the mud, and his socks had rotted off, along with some of his skin. He lived on cold Spam and struggled to keep his mind from drifting into madness.

One day the battle eased enough that he could crawl out of the trench and read his mail, which included a care package from his home church. Hoping for some candy or a good book, he tore open the package to find a beautiful necktie. "I had no shoes," he said, "but I was the best-dressed man in the trench."

Thank You, Lord, for the men and women who have served our country—
and for the safety valve of humor, a wonderful gift.
—DANIEL SCHANTZ

So do not throw away your confidence; it will be richly rewarded.
—HEBREWS 10:35 (NIV)

Everything I thought about on my morning walk made me worry. Biggest was that my husband Gordon had come home, saying that he wanted to put his name in the hat for a job in another city. Everything inside of me screamed, *No, I don't want to move again! I don't have the time or energy for it!* "It would disrupt my whole life," I told him. As I rounded the curve and headed home, I tried to lift my problems to God, but somehow it didn't seem to do any good.

I collapsed in the living room and opened my Bible. All at once, a sentence in Hebrews electrified me. I hurried upstairs to copy it down in my journal in capital letters. "DO NOT THROW AWAY YOUR CONFIDENCE."

"Is that the only way confidence can be lost—if I throw it away myself?" I wrote. "That's an amazing thought. Usually I think that overwhelming circumstances or my own lack of ability or the way others have treated me robs me of my confidence. What if confidence is really mine and mine alone, either to keep or throw away?"

In the past, I'd often mentally substituted the word *self-confidence* for *confidence* when reading the Bible. Self-confidence is not always possible or practical because there are many things beyond my ability and control. But Hebrews tells me to place my trust and reliance on God, "for he who promised is faithful" (Hebrews 10:23, NIV).

The next morning, as I rounded the same curve in my morning walk, I smiled. Every time worry or depression crept in, I would simply remind myself, "Do not throw away your confidence." I went about my day with assurance and optimism.

I began praying for whatever God thought best concerning Gordon's future job, even if it meant laying aside my desire for stability. And I prayed with confidence because I was sure that whatever God's plan, it would be so much better than mine.

Lord, instead of throwing away my confidence, help me to throw my whole heart into trusting You.
—KAREN BARBER

I even found great pleasure in hard work, an additional reward for all my labors.

—ECCLESIASTES 2:10 (NLT)

TODAY'S DATE: _____

Lord, I ask for the dedication and energy I need to give my very best effort to the labor You've provided for me.

—JOSHUA SUNDQUIST

I will lift up mine eyes unto the hills, from whence cometh my help.

—PSALM 121:1

TODAY'S DATE: _____

Dear God, thank You for helping me to ignore the rocks and cactus while I run with You!

—TIM WILLIAMS

Daily Guideposts: Reflections for a Faith-Filled Life

Daily Guideposts Journal is just one of the resources Guideposts offers to help you make the most of your devotional time. Other books include:

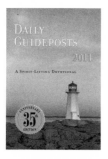

DAILY GUIDEPOSTS 2011

Now in its thirty-fifth annual edition, America's favorite devotional has helped millions of readers to a closer walk with God and a richer, fuller life. For every day of 2011, you'll find a short Scripture verse, a first-person story and a brief prayer for every day of the year. It's available in regular-print jacketed hardcover and deluxe faux-leather with gilded edges (432 pages), and large-print paperback (624 pages).

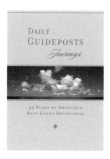

DAILY GUIDEPOSTS JOURNEYS

This special collection of more than one hundred devotionals brings together the best of thirty-five years of *Daily Guideposts*, enriched with a year-by-year history of the *Daily Guideposts* family and the events that have shaped us all. It's available in jacketed hardcover (304 pages).

All of these books are available at your local bookseller
or direct from Guideposts at www.shopguideposts.com.

DAILY GUIDEPOSTS CIRCLE OF FRIENDS

Join our circle of friends and receive practical help to make your devotional life deeper and richer. Benefits include an exclusive Web site, quarterly newsletter, weekly e-mails from *Daily Guideposts* writers and a bonus devotional book. For more information, visit www.dailyguideposts.com/circleoffriends or write to *Daily Guideposts* Circle of Friends, PO Box 5864, Harlan, Iowa 52593.